11962

S0-BGQ-956

African Success Story
The Ivory Coast

Marc and Evelyne Bernheim

At a time when most of the new nations of
Africa are suffering painfully disruptive birth
pangs, the Ivory Coast stands out as a notable
exception. Since its peaceful independence from
France in 1960, it has become a stable, pros-
perous member of the world community. A
small country of only a few million people, it is
now among the world's top producers of cocoa,
pineapple, coffee, and bananas, which—along
with the new industries these crops have stimu-
lated—bring Ivorians one of the highest per
capita incomes in Black Africa. People flock to
Abidjan, the capital city, not only from the
farms and villages of the Ivory Coast but from
the poorer countries of Africa as well, to work
in the factories and government offices and,
increasingly, to attend school and university.

This remarkable development has come
about in large part through the thoughtful,
cautious leadership of Felix Houphouet-Boigny,
his country's first President. His story, the
Ivory Coast's history as a colony, its hopes
and plans for the future, and the ways in which
the Ivorians themselves are affected by the
enormous changes taking place in their world
are all part of the fascinating picture Marc and
Evelyne Bernheim project of this emerging nation. As in the companion volume, *From Bush
to City: A Look at the New Africa*, their excitement with the place and its many peoples is
infectious. In succinct, informative text, gen-
erously illustrated with striking black-and-
white photographs, they have again provided
dramatic insight into modern Africa.

AFRICAN SUCCESS STORY

The Ivory Coast

Marc and Evelyne Bernheim

HARCOURT, BRACE & WORLD, INC.

New York

To Jean Fritz

also by Marc and Evelyne Bernheim
FROM BUSH TO CITY: A Look at the New Africa

FRONTISPIECE PHOTOGRAPH: Women's club dances for the President at his Abidjan palace on New Year's Day.

FIRST EDITION

Library of Congress Catalog Card Number: 72-84772

PRINTED IN THE UNITED STATES OF AMERICA

Contents

1   African Success Story   7

2   Under the French   15

3   One Leader Rises   27

4   Abidjan, Boomtown   39

5   A Country of Planters   49

6   Generation Gap   61

7   Heritage   81

   Index   96

1

African Success Story

Success stories are rare in struggling Africa. Thirty-nine new nations plunged into independence in the 1960's with great expectations. For half a century, colonial powers had governed them, stopped tribal wars, built roads, schools, and hospitals, developed their economy and pushed new crops, but they also brought great sufferings and imposed on African peoples an alien culture, a foreign religion, a restless way of life. Independence would bring the end of all hardships, many African leaders promised.

A decade after independence, some of the growing pains have erupted into revolutions, some of the tribal hatreds have exploded into wars. Too many new nations are still troubled, mismanaged, or desperately poor.

One small nation of West Africa stands out as an exception. Without causing any headlines, the Ivory Coast has quietly grown into Black Africa's showcase for success.

Formerly one of France's seventeen African colonies, it became independent in 1960. About the size of New Mexico, its 124,000 square miles have become an oasis of well-being surrounded by five envious neighbors: Guinea and Liberia to the west, Ghana to the east, Mali and Upper Volta to the north.

Fascinated youngsters watch a helicopter bringing VIP's from the airport to town.

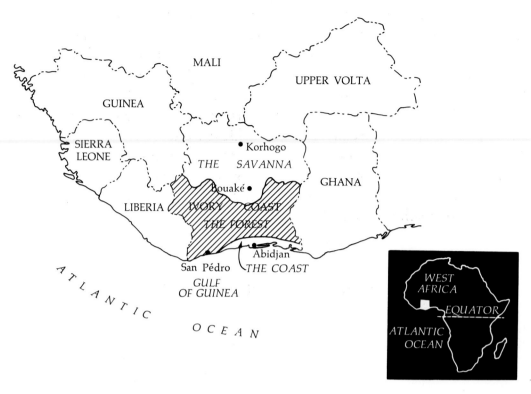

Surrounded by five West African neighbors, the Ivory Coast has three zones running east-west: the northern savanna, the forest, and the coast.

The Ivory Coast headed for independence with much the same problems its African neighbors faced. It had many distinct tribes, still somewhat uneasy with each other. It had an unevenly developed country, a small, educated elite, and thousands of teen-agers, unhappy with village life, flocking to the city, yet unprepared for city ways.

What makes this nation so different? Why has it succeeded when so many others still search for a better way?

The Ivory Coast has put all its efforts into building up prosperity at home. It has kept out of the news, offending no one, yet allowing no outside interference in its own affairs. Unlike Guinea, it has made no hot-headed pronouncements against the West; it did not angrily break with France. It has not thrown out Peace Corps volunteers or courted the Russians and then lived to regret it. Unlike Ghana or Mali, it has not been living beyond its means. And unlike Nigeria, for so long considered Africa's most promising nation, it has not allowed tribal rivalries to flare into war.

The story of this successful African country is really one of contradictions. It was for years a neglected colony. The first generation of Ivorian children entered primary school when both Ghana and Senegal already had university graduates. When it became independent, it started with no greater potentials than Guinea, Ghana, or Nigeria. Surprisingly, the Ivory Coast has surpassed most Black African nations economically and has achieved one of the highest per capita incomes of all Black Africa. Its economy keeps growing at the rate of 9 percent a year. The country is doing so well that it has attracted over 800,000 people—one-fifth of the total population—from poorer neighbor countries.

The savanna, least developed of the three zones, still has mud-hut villages, many isolated and unchanged.

This prosperity, a fragile treasure, is due not only to the country's natural resources, but also to the wise and strong leadership of the president. Félix Houphouet-Boigny has backed up his country's existing wealth with a steady flow of French, other European, and, recently, American investments. He has inspired, perhaps more successfully than any other African leader, the foreign investors' confidence, and he has never yet made them regret their trust.

He has been criticized, however, often severely, by younger and more radical Africans. In 1957, the Ivory Coast was still attached to France. Kwame Nkrumah came for a visit just a few days after leading his own country, Ghana, to independence from Great Britain.

Abidjan, the capital, built around lagoons, has become Africa's boomtown.

The coast: almost four hundred miles of fishing villages, coconut groves, and lagoons.

Both leaders had tremendous ambitions, but Nkrumah had always been an impatient man. Having obtained Ghana's freedom, he was obsessed with another dream: to found a United States of Africa, which he hoped to lead. He strongly urged Houphouet-Boigny to break away from France, but Houphouet disagreed. He had worked for years to build up a strong, stable country. He wanted to secure the well-being of his people first. Better to postpone independence by just a few more years, he thought, and in the meantime get France to further strengthen his country with even larger investments.

Nkrumah accused him of being far too cautious. As the two leaders parted, Houphouet-Boigny challenged the Ghanaian: "The die is cast," he said. "Let now God, Providence and the work of men determine the future of each of our experiments. . . . We have chosen different paths. In ten years' time we will compare the results we have obtained."

Unfortunately, Nkrumah could not keep this date. A year before the meeting was due, he was overthrown by his own army for having squandered Ghana's great wealth on personal political schemes. Today Nkrumah is exiled in Guinea, while Ghana is trying to repay the enormous debts he incurred.

Meanwhile, Houphouet-Boigny stuck to his plan. He waited three years and then led the Ivory Coast to independence. His timing was perfect. His country was strong.

Over the years, even the most radical African leaders who had criticized Houphouet-Boigny have come to see this prosperity for themselves. Intrigued by the Ivory Coast's success, they tour the country, are impressed, and in their farewell speeches hint that perhaps Houphouet-Boigny's way, for all its cautious conservatism, may be the wiser.

Because it has achieved success the quiet way, the Ivory Coast is hardly known in the United States. The sixteenth century Dutch bought tusks here and gave it this name, which has remained, though today most elephants have disappeared. The Ivory Coast has a population of 4.4 million, belonging to over sixty tribal groups. Some are affluent planters. They own trucks and large bank accounts. They are progressive, yet immensely proud of their ancestors' gold crowns and scepters, which they take to yam festivals. Some are city people who had to give up the old traditions to try and fit into an often bewildering new world. Some are northern farmers who still remain in almost medieval villages and fear the change that is touching the entire country and threatening to topple their tight-knit society. They still carve statues, stark as the savanna landscape, and in their sacred groves they still wear long fire-spitter masks at rites no outsider may see. Some are educators and ministers, part of the very small elite. And some are restless teen-agers who grew up with independence. They idealize younger African leaders who may not have accomplished half as much as Houphouet-Boigny has for his people. They grow up in cities or want to live in them. How has change and prosperity affected these vastly dissimilar people?

The lush forest, up to 150 miles deep, runs through the center of the country.

2

Under the French

"Ten pieces of assorted cloth, one barrel of brandy, five white hats, two mirrors, one grind organ . . ." From now on France was to make this yearly payment to King Peter of Assinie in exchange for his land and river at Grand Bassam. On February 9, 1842, Peter and his elders signed the parchment treaty with crosses, having been persuaded that it was "in their interest to open trade relations with a rich and kind people and to place themselves under the sovereignty of their powerful monarch . . . His Majesty Louis Philippe I, King of the French."

Why had no Europeans settled here before? Ever since the fifteenth century, the Portuguese, the Dutch, the French, the British had built forts up and down the West African coast and traded their glass beads and rusty guns for gold, ivory, spices, and, later on, slaves.

This part of the coast had little to offer. Occasionally a caravel would anchor, buy some peppers, replenish its fresh water supply, and promptly sail on, for the humidity was unbearable. If a seaman was lucky enough to escape yellow fever, he was bound to come down with malarial chills. Besides, parts of the coast were inaccessible. Only the natives with their swift canoes could cross seven-foot surf, marshy inlets, rivers clogged with rocks and mangrove thickets.

Except for plastic buckets and enamel pans, this isolated market in the northern Ivory Coast has changed little from early colonial days.

Soon even the adventurous Portuguese lost interest when navigators began spreading rumors of cannibalism. A long strip became known as the "Mean Peoples' Coast." So trading vessels stayed safely anchored at sea. The merchandise was neatly laid out on deck, converting the ship into a bazaar. Three cannon shots opened the trade. The natives would paddle out, climb aboard, and sometimes take all day to barter their gold or ivory tusks for bugles, cheap calicoes, and feathered hats.

Traditional method of storing maize in a tree to protect it from rodents was in use before the French came.

So was the system of weaving among the Senufo people of the savanna.

A short strip to the east of the "Mean Peoples' Coast" became known as the "Good Peoples' Coast," but France was too busy with continental wars to get involved. For centuries no one really took the Ivory Coast seriously—until Bouet-Villaumez came along. This young French naval officer persuaded coastal rulers to sign treaties of alliance with France in return for her "protection" and a payment of beads, guns, and brandy. Back home, he so praised the potential wealth of this strange land that a few of his countrymen finally decided to set up shop there. No one realized that the coastal kings he had befriended had no authority over forest tribes. One trader ventured beyond the lagoons and returned stripped of all his goods. He was lucky to get out alive. After him no Frenchman dared penetrate the forest—not till the very end of the nineteenth century.

Who lived there? "Little hairy people," according to tribal legends, reddish brown, pygmy-like. But had the white man dared go beyond the lagoons, he would have met normal-sized tribesmen who had migrated from east and west and had taken refuge in this forest in the seventeenth and eighteenth centuries. The Akan tribes, by far the largest group, had fled from domination by the fierce Ashanti warriors of present-day Ghana. The refugees, in turn, enslaved those who stood in their path or pushed them out. Each forest tribe jealously guarded its own territory set apart by large patches of no-man's-land where only elephants roamed.

Not far from these loosely shaped societies were several kingdoms so well organized that every member belonged to a caste and had a precise role to play. Slaves were used to pan gold dust that was sold to Moslems in the north, as well as to Europeans on the coast. Minstrels were hired to recite great tribal events, as there was no written language in any of these societies. There were jesters to amuse the king and noblemen to advise him. Kingmakers elected him. Once in power, the king was considered sacred, but if he abused the people's trust, elders and priests could dethrone him.

It was this forbidding forest, the bad reputation of its tribes, and the lack of natural harbors that spared the Ivory Coast from most of the European slave trade. To get slaves for the white man's ships, a trader had to enter the forest thoroughly armed. He could be ambushed along any footpath and relieved of his mirrors and brandy. Or he could be captured himself and sold to some local kingdom for

In a forest village, mother and aunt prepare a young girl for the same ceremony their great-grandmothers participated in.

Fly whisks and handkerchiefs swing in little girls' hands at an Abouré year-end dance.

Drums are beaten at a village funeral by Senufo youngsters of Korhogo.

Xylophones are played by recently initiated boys in a savanna village.

twelve thousand kola nuts. Hardly a coastal trader was willing to take those risks. Gradually, slave ships stopped coming to the Ivory Coast for "merchandise" they could get from the strong warrior societies of Ghana, Dahomey, and Nigeria. In the eighteenth century, at the very height of the slave trade, less than two thousand slaves a year were taken from the Ivory Coast, compared to 100,000 yearly from Nigeria.

By the mid-nineteenth century, France was ready to give up the Ivory Coast where her trading posts had failed. Most French firms packed up and left, but one merchant held on.

Arthur Verdier from La Rochelle was delighted to see his competitors go: now he could have the market all to himself. But he stayed not only to boost his own trading schemes. Something about the Ivory Coast had excited him from the very beginning. He started to look for gold mines; he initiated coffee and cocoa plantations,

often out of his own pocket. The climate was miserable, Verdier admitted, but this was, in his opinion, no reason to neglect the Ivory Coast. France named him official Resident in 1878, yet gave him little encouragement otherwise. With a meager subsidy and a tiny police force, Verdier managed to keep the French flag flying in the Ivory Coast despite France's lack of faith.

He did not have to hold on alone much longer. The Berlin Conference Treaty of 1885 now required all European powers with interests in Africa to occupy the areas they claimed. France resumed control of the trading posts she had abandoned for twenty years. Having recovered from the Franco-German War, she was ready for "colonial adventure." She sent explorers to the hinterlands to extend her position beyond the narrow coastal strip. In 1893, she officially declared the Ivory Coast a colony, then proceeded to draw up borders to separate it from the British Gold Coast and from Liberia. She created administrative posts up north and put Louis-Gustave Binger—a former explorer—in charge of the new colony and of its peaceful occupation.

Little was known of the hinterland. Young officers, bored with nineteenth century France, willingly took up this challenge. They longed to be the first white men to "open up" an unknown Africa. They set out in little groups on haphazard expeditions. They walked with their porters every one of those hundreds of miles, with mud to their hips, weakened by malaria, sick with yellow fever, plagued with the endless stings of infinitely small insects. They followed tracks that narrowed, disappeared, and sometimes ended in a sudden maze of giant grasses. They crossed turbulent rapids to villages that had no food for them or even sent hostile warriors out to meet them. Yet the tremendous pride of personally representing a great empire to the chiefs who received them with honor made those young men forget their months of suffering and fall in love with Africa. Binger himself admitted it: "In Africa," he wrote in his diary, "man really feels he is someone. . . . To suffer once in a while is still the best way to feel alive."

Something happened to help the French occupation: Samory Touré, a Moslem warlord from Guinea, descended on the northern tribes, raiding them for slaves and tribute. The terrified tribes ran for help to the French troops, who captured the warlord and took over.

Minstrel to the Boundiali chief recites tribal history dating back to the time when no white man was in the land.

On the coast the new colony grew peacefully but very slowly, for France still spent as little as possible. "We could not, at least for the time being, have teachers," Binger complained. He asked his customs men to start a school. "You will take boys and girls, after the hot hours, and when your other duties will permit, you will walk the children on the beach, in the village, in the bush, and you will do your best to have them learn the names of everything. . . . Then teach them opposite adjectives: big and small . . . good and bad . . . verbs, starting with the imperative. . . . When they will know all that, plus the greetings and marks of respect, then we shall see."

So the colony would be self-supporting, France pushed new crops —cocoa and coffee—and encouraged Frenchmen to settle there and develop an export trade. Seven hundred and thirty-five Frenchmen had arrived by 1905 and soon prospered.

But very few administrators who succeeded Binger had his understanding of Africans. One governor would send troops to wipe out the inland trouble spots and compel forest tribes to grow the crops France needed. Another imposed forced labor to get roads built and plantations started. Villages that failed to comply would have their yam crops destroyed, their huts burned, their chiefs jailed or exiled. Yet tribal wars were stopped. The new schools were free and so was vaccination. But in those days, hardly any tribesman wanted his son in school, and everyone feared the white man's needle.

Just before World War II, relations between French and Ivorians did improve. Young teachers and civil servants, sent over by a more liberal French administration, behaved as friends, not as superiors. They invited Ivorians to their homes. Behind closed doors, Ivorian students and junior clerks poured out all the bitterness that had piled up for so long, grievances they had been unable to speak of before. They complained about the "little French," the city shopkeepers, the truck drivers who had come over to Africa on a one-way ticket, hoping to make quick money. They were the ones who practiced racial discrimination. The African farmers had complaints, too. French planters and traders were squeezing them out of business.

Under this new French administration, Ivorians were not just listened to. They were encouraged to form political groups and trade unions. But the good times lasted only a few years.

When France fell to the Germans in 1940, the Africans did not know what to expect. She had dominated them for half a century. Now she herself was surrendering to the Nazis. Would her colonies fall under German rule as well? Students and chiefs looked up to General de Gaulle, head of the French government in exile, as "the only true Frenchman," but French West Africa was held firmly by the Vichy government of Marshall Pétain and subjected to the harshest economic burdens she had ever born. Every region was forced to contribute all its crops without pay. There were no trucks, no fuel, Even lagoon boats were paralyzed. Porters were rounded up by force to carry the contributions of coffee, cocoa, and palm kernels sometimes for hundreds of miles to the railway line. Small farmers who had been forced to grow cocoa and had given up raising their traditional food crops went hungry for the first time in their lives. And all this hardship was caused by someone else's war taking place thousands of miles away.

Nazi theories of a superior race were extended to Africa by the French wartime administration. In Abidjan, Africans were made to sign a declaration stating that they were not Jews. They could no longer enter European hotels. They had to be served at special counters in department stores. Anyone attending a meeting of more than twenty-five people was arrested. Anyone suspected of secretly helping de Gaulle's cause was watched by police. There was no freedom of speech, no way of forming a political party. The suffering seemed all the more bitter to those who had experienced so much kindness from the previous administration. France, whose ideals of "Liberty, Equality, Fraternity" every African schoolboy had memorized, was suddenly practicing racial discrimination in her own colony. "Is *this* the France we learned to admire so much?" an Ivorian student asked.

3

One Leader Rises

World War II was ending. African soldiers who had fought in
France's army had seen her nearly crushed by Nazi Germany, on
her own soil. They had made other eye-opening discoveries. They
saw white men sweeping gutters. They saw them emptying garbage,
even begging. This was unheard of in Africa, where the white man
still ruled, where only the African held the broom. In the French
army, Africans also learned that every soldier—black or white—
could work his way up by his own efforts. Now these veterans were
coming home with medals and generous pensions from France. They
were filled with hope and a kinder impression of the white man's
world. But in the Ivory Coast, a tight-knit community of French
settlers was still practicing racial discrimination and forced labor
as if nothing had changed.

In 1944 Charles de Gaulle, then heading the French provisional
government, made a pledge to Africa. He spoke of granting the
colonies greater autonomy to reward them for having rallied to his
cause two years earlier. He promised them representation in the
Paris Parliament. He spoke of creating new industries, new jobs, new
schools, so badly needed in French-speaking Africa. By the end of
the war, the Ivory Coast had only four university graduates.

Félix Houphouet-Boigny, former doctor, planter, and Baoulé chief, pulled his country
through crisis with nonviolent methods.

Government leaders step past palace guards to call on the President.

Gardeners prepare the grounds of the presidential palace—a gift from France to the newly independent Ivory Coast.

Lead lion from France guards the gates of the administrative section.

Bronze dancers from Italy lead to the reception wing.

That same year, de Gaulle sent a sympathetic governor to Abidjan: André Latrille was ready to help the Africans, even if this meant antagonizing the local French.

The real trouble went on in the bush. Two hundred and fifty French planters produced over one-third of the cocoa and the coffee in the entire country. They had the best crops, which always sold at the highest prices to French trading firms. The small, five-acre African planter was desperate. Too poor to buy a truck and transport his beans to town, he was at the mercy of French or Lebanese middlemen who went around his village and bought his beans at prices that hurt.

African planters tried to fight back. Some toured the forest region making fiery speeches. Others spoke of forming a union. Only one planter had a plan—the least dramatic speaker of all. Forced labor must be abolished, Félix Houphouet suggested. Replace it with voluntary labor. Get rid of the middleman. Sign contracts directly with the trading firms, he urged, and they will buy our crops at a decent price.

Who was this gentle man? "He had the salvation of Africa about him," an early follower recalled. He had a gift for putting people at ease, but he also had an iron will. At thirty-nine, he was the most educated of all Ivorians. He was a doctor, a planter, and a Baoulé chief. His patients were planters, too. They suffered as much as he did from French exploitation. They confided in him. They urged him to give up his medical career and form a planters' union.

In less than a year, with the governor's help, Houphouet organized twenty thousand planters and laborers, then transformed this union into the country's first political party. He campaigned in the remotest villages. Illiterate chiefs barely understood Houphouet's plan—but one thing was clear: this man was going to fight for the end of forced labor.

All over the country, chiefs had to supply men to work on road gangs and European plantations. Those who got warning in time would flee to the neighboring Gold Coast. But guards caught most villages by surprise. They would encircle the huts. They would round up all able-bodied men. They would march them out silently, cracking their whips on anyone who tried to escape. "You should have seen . . . African planters forced to abandon their own farms to work for starvation wages," Houphouet recalled, "seen the recruiting

31

agents . . . modern slave traders, push people . . . into trucks, or lock them up in baggage cars like animals . . . seen the old women begging to keep their sons, their only source of support . . . to understand the drama of forced labor in the Ivory Coast."

Houphouet was elected to represent his country at the 1945 Paris National Assembly. The French Socialists and Communists were interested in what he had to say. They were willing to help him. With their support, he proposed a bill in March, 1946, to abolish forced labor in overseas France. "Monsieur Houphouet's law" passed without any opposition.

Overnight, his name traveled all over the bush. Everyone called him "Liberator." Thousands of forced laborers deserted the French plantations and drowned their years of suffering in palm wine. Drums that had played only for funerals now burst out with joy. Storytellers talked of Brother Houphouet who won the Battle of Forced Labor in the White Man's Parliament. Everyone rushed to the market stands to buy little flasks of Houphouet perfume, to buy Houphouet cloth printed with his portrait.

The man who had left Abidjan as a very junior deputy now came back a triumphant hero. He rode into town side by side with the French governor. Soon he was elected president of the new democratic party, which had grown out of the old planters' union and of a giant party that rallied other French West African groups.

His hold on the people was assured. Still, he could not accomplish anything for them by staying home. Frenchmen ran his country. Even the governor took orders from Paris. Houphouet knew he had to stay near the seat of power. He had to become one of the lawmakers in the French Parliament. Only then could he lobby for reforms that would bring greater freedom to the people of Africa.

Before the November, 1946, assembly, Deputy Houphouet added "Boigny" to his name. In the Baoulé tribal language, it means "irresistible force."

But this time, Houphouet met with a very different reception in Paris. By 1947 France was involved with a war in Vietnam, with riots in North Africa, with strikes in her own cities. She was in no mood to grant any more liberties to Black Africa. De Gaulle had resigned, and the French lawmakers now watered down most of his liberal proposals.

Governor Latrille was recalled from the Ivory Coast. He was replaced by harsh administrators who mistook Houphouet-Boigny for a trouble-making Communist. None of them realized that he was only using leftist help to get his party organized and strengthened.

The worst of all the governors arrived in 1948. Laurent Péchoux was determined to break Houphouet-Boigny. He built up opposition parties. He openly bribed Ivorians to defect to them. When they refused, he arrested them. He played up tribal hatreds. The people looked to their leader for guidance. Stirred up by Communist agents, workers wanted to revolt against the governor, but Houphouet-Boigny held them back. He would allow no violence in his country. He would give France no excuse to pass even harsher laws.

And so, demonstrations remained peaceful—until the day government troops started firing at demonstrating crowds. The bloodshed caused by the governor grew, and France did nothing to stop it. In Paris, no one would listen to Houphouet-Boigny. By now his leftist allies were in the opposition, and their agents in Africa were trying to wreck Houphouet-Boigny's peaceful tactics.

The riots were hurting the country's economy. Plantations that had produced six thousand tons of coffee in one year now yielded nothing at all. Farmers, white and black, were too busy demonstrating to harvest their crops. They all desperately needed peace.

To regain influence in Paris, Houphouet was forced to do something dramatic. He broke with the leftists and joined the conservatives in power. From that moment on, he was no longer considered a "dangerous leftist." Houphouet had made his peace with France. Now she made her peace with him.

The governor was recalled in 1951. Instantly the riots stopped.

New surveys confirmed that the Ivory Coast was one of the most promising countries of French West Africa. French businessmen began to pour investments into Houphouet's country. The Korean War was boosting the price of lumber, rubber, coffee, and cocoa, its major crops. By 1956, the Ivory Coast had become the richest of all French West African territories. This spectacular boom gave Houphouet-Boigny a tremendous feeling of confidence. He was determined not to let this first wave of prosperity go. He was determined to make his country the economic showcase of Black Africa.

By now he had attained the highest rank any African had ever reached in the French government: he was a cabinet minister. He used this position to get a law passed granting new civil rights to all French-speaking Africa, including—at last—universal suffrage.

But in Guinea and Mali, people were anxious for change. They were jobless, landless. Their leaders were talking about demanding independence from France. Houphouet had no reason to share their restlessness. His people were prospering. Their land was good. Prices for crops were high. France was not only the Ivory Coast's best customer: she was also its first investor. A break with the mother country now, Houphouet feared, might stop the prosperity he had worked so hard to achieve.

Other African leaders criticized him for being too cautious. "We count in the Ivory Coast twenty lawyers, ten doctors, three engineers," he replied. "Do you think we can get along without France?" In two or three years' time, his country would be stronger and ready to stand on its own. For the moment, he urged his neighbors to maintain strong links with France.

When Ghana became independent the following year, 1957, the restlessness started all over again. Ghana was the first Black African nation to be free while her neighbors still remained tightly wrapped in Mother France's old-fashioned coat. True, France did hand out a few concessions, but she still controlled their economy, their defenses, their foreign policy. Leopold Senghor, the poet-president of Senegal, aptly described her behavior as "a kind of hesitation waltz, in which you move two steps forward to go one step back, and in which the left hand takes back half of what the right hand gave."

When de Gaulle returned to power in 1958, he loosened the French grip over Africa. He shaped a new French Community in which France would be the senior partner. Her African possessions would become self-governing republics. They would be able to vote for complete independence soon.

De Gaulle's plan was a wise one—Houphouet and most of his neighbors agreed. Everyone would maintain ties with France for just a few more years. Everyone but Sekou Touré of Guinea: he would rather eat boiled manioc in freedom, he shouted, than buttered bread in bondage. He insulted Houphouet; he insulted de Gaulle. Without a word, France gave Guinea the independence Sekou Touré demanded. Overnight, de Gaulle recalled all French technicians and

The first lady, Thérèse Houphouet-Boigny.

withdrew all aid. Overnight, Guinea's promising economy (with her mineral wealth she was potentially an even richer country than the Ivory Coast) collapsed. Thousands of her citizens migrated to Abidjan in search of jobs and a happier life. Thousands still do.

In 1960, Houphouet-Boigny asked France for independence. She granted it gracefully, sponsored the Ivory Coast's admission to the United Nations, and even increased her aid to the new republic. Houphouet-Boigny had cut the colonial apron strings tactfully.

Back home his people were frantic with excitement. Independence would bring a magic world—the end to taxes, they hoped, the end to all the hardships they had ever known. In Abidjan, newspaper boys discussed how their country was taking its seat at the U.N., what colors the new flag would be, which of their countrymen would replace Frenchmen in the new government.

To Houphouet-Boigny, independence meant a calm and orderly transfer of power. And so it was.

Women's club carries the President's banner into the palace and dances for him on New Year's Day.

Today he is both president of the nation and head of the only political party. His way of taming the opposition is to invite his critics to join the party, thus keeping them under control. While he was visiting the United States in 1962, Americans asked him how he could reconcile the Western idea of democracy with his version of one-man, one-party rule. "We are a young country," he replied. "These are still the beginnings of our political life . . ."

The Ivory coast is barely ten years old. Houphouet-Boigny has seen France weakened, often paralyzed by too many parties. He believes his country is not yet strong enough to afford them. Right now his aim is to mold the over sixty distrustful tribes into one solidly united nation.

To middle-aged Ivorians, Houphouet is "Father of the Nation." But the young people grew up with independence. They did not know Houphouet the fighter, Houphouet the hero. They are drawn to flashier leaders who have not accomplished half as much for their people. They criticize him for still keeping too many French advisers around, for not Africanizing jobs faster, for his nine-million-dollar palace. They have called it "out of place," yet they forget it was a gift of France to the new republic. They fail to see that the prosperity Houphouet-Boigny worked for has transformed Abidjan into a boomtown. Now this palace no longer seems out of proportion.

On New Year's Day, ambassadors, church leaders, and all the government members come to the palace to greet him. They toast "The Boss" with speeches and champagne under the crystal chandeliers. In the afternoon, the marble halls suddenly shed their French formality. Thousands of tribesmen file in at the gates to present their wishes to the Chief of all Tribes. Troubadours sing out his praise through wooden masks. Stilt acrobats from the northwest flex their muscles. Dancers twirl and toss slim girls over tall sabers. Tam-tams and rattles speak their own, still stronger soul-language, transporting the visitor back to some medieval forest kingdom where courtiers paid homage to their king.

4

Abidjan, Boomtown

A jet pierces the swollen rain clouds of a November sky. The newcomer stares out to catch a glimpse of the city. At first he sees only murky lagoons and fishermen standing in canoes, unwinding their nets, not even looking up. Beyond, he sees an endless forest, broken up here and there by a rusty-roofed village.

Suddenly, as the plane circles down and around the lagoon, he discovers glittering buildings piercing the shapeless dark green rain forest, like a mirage. Just as the plane is about to land, he notices the giant five-part harbor connected by bridges to downtown sections. He is amazed. Buildings here are not squeezed tight, helter-skelter, in the middle of an immovable shantytown as in Accra or Lagos or any other older African city. These buildings breathe freely surrounded by wide boulevards and pleasing plazas. Everything here is planned and stretched around the curving lagoon. On all sides, rows of apartment houses stand like a thousand neatly aligned dominoes and push the forest out.

As the visitor steps out of the brand-new, air-conditioned airport, still dazed from the night flight, he will find himself standing in 95° heat, surrounded by a crowd of haggling cab drivers who try to grab

Factory workers cycle across Houphouet-Boigny Bridge.

him or his luggage. The driver who has picked him goes too fast; his radio blares too loud. "Cotton in your field means gold in your pocket," the announcer tells listeners in the bush. He goes on to report that cocoa, the Ivory Coast's second export crop has hit a new high on the world market. "Lucky country," the driver comments. "That's why I left Guinea. This is where the money is."

The highway glistens with rain puddles. All of Africa seems to be walking along that airport road to town. Herdboys wash their skinny sheep in the lagoon. Nomads from Niger gather their grumbling cows. They call them with endearing click-sounds and tap on their long curved horns with sticks to assemble them for auction. Near the first factories, women hop-walk to market balancing gallons of bubbly palm wine on their heads. Middle-class Africans whiz by in neat French cars, bought on credit. Near the instant coffee plant, laundrymen from the north flatten patches of bright cotton cloth washed in the rivulets. Workers are crowding in at the factories' gates. On the side paths of the Houphouet-Boigny Bridge, cyclists frantically ring their bells trying to squeeze in between school-children carrying books and ink bottles on their heads. A politician cruises by in his black air-conditioned Mercedes.

By now the cab has crossed Houphouet-Boigny Bridge. It winds around the oval plaza, whose center is decorated with a French sculptor's symbol for the Ivory Coast: a bronze young woman slightly leaning forward to present her varied fruits on a platter. The visitor rides through downtown Abidjan, past the President's palace, past the ministries and City Hall, past the carefully clipped lawns of Parliament, past the President's private villa shaped like a control tower and overlooking his ministers' homes in the middle of the residential section where successful Africans and Europeans live.

Finally the cab stops at a luxury hotel, complete with sauna club, bowling alley, French pastry shop, American snack bar—even a skating rink. Can this be Africa? Outside, between two swimming pools, a giant cottonwood left over from the rain forest stands facing the skyline of Abidjan. It is the sacred tree housing the ancestors' souls. The builders did not dare remove it, for it belongs to the little fishing village at the bottom of the hill.

The village world, though so close, never crosses the hotel world except when a helicopter lands on the swimming pool lawn. Then mothers tuck their babies into their cloths and run up the hill to watch, breathless and fascinated.

In 1900, there was no city. There were only three or four fishing villages, similar to this one, clustered around the lagoon. Seven hundred fishermen lived here. It was not until the 1930's that this was thought to be a suitable place for a capital. By then, a railroad was bringing crops from the hinterland to ships waiting at the coast. It also brought northern tribesmen who, unlike the forest people, did not mind hard manual labor and were put to work clearing the forest. Ten thousand came to live here. The Governor and the entire European community moved in from their former capital of Bingerville. One after another, the European firms set up their warehouses.

Abidjan today is seven jet hours from New York, but in colonial times it seemed like the end of the world to the European agents who came to represent the trading companies.

"You are a lucky devil!" a Londoner wrote to his young friend who was coming here for a British firm. "You are off to a land of golden sunshine, blue skies, shady palms, and iced drinks." How different he found the reality! Abidjan was so hot, so humid that he built his bungalow close enough to the office to walk home and change his soaking shirt several times a day. After business hours, he might have dinner at another agent's house, and on Christmas Eve eat turkey and truffles at the Governor's. But most nights he would simply stay home to write long, fond letters to his wife. Clouds of insects swarmed around the kerosene lamp. His houseboy would stand waving a large wicker fan, but the air he moved was still sweltering.

It was not until 1951 that Abidjan began to even vaguely resemble the city it is today. A canal linking the inland lagoons to the sea converted Abidjan into a deep-water port at last. Now cargo ships could sail right into the city and almost up to the railway terminal. Thousands of tribesmen arrived, not only from the bush but also from all the neighboring countries, to hire themselves out as construction workers and harbor hands.

Today, Abidjan has grown into the largest city of French-speaking West Africa, with a population of 450,000. Thousands of young

A mother selects toys in a department store.

Fishermen from a nearby lagoon village paddle by one of the city hotels.

Office workers buy evening papers at a newsstand in downtown Abidjan.

tribesmen still leave their peaceful villages for the "Paris of Africa." Do they find what they want here?

Kipré is a twenty-five-year-old Bété tribesman who arrived in Abidjan six years ago. His story is typical. He had been happy in his father's compound until he went to school. After five years of school, the village seemed too small for him. Nothing seemed right any more. Not only did he have to work on his father's coffee plantation; he also had to help in his uncles' fields. They were illiterate, yet they were his elders. He kept having arguments with them. Truly, he felt, this was a waste of time.

And so, at age twenty, Kipré left his wife and children behind and boarded a truck for Abidjan. At first, he lived with a cousin in the

Barbershops in a low income section of Abidjan

city. He went from firm to firm looking for a job. He could have found a factory job without too much trouble. But Kipré wanted to sit at a desk.

A new export firm opened up, and they needed a clerk. It was not exactly the glamorous career he had dreamed of. He would have to get papers signed and delivered all over town. But at least it was a white-collar job, and he would be working in an office.

He took this job, and soon his family joined him. They all moved into one of six hundred ground-floor flats that had been completed in the working-class section.

From the front, Kipré's three-room home not only looks like all the neighbors'; it also could be in any working-class section anywhere in the world. But in the backyard, life is just as it was in the village, except for the water faucet and the light bulb. Here Kipré's wife washes the baby in an enamel basin; she pounds plantains in the mortar; she cooks on a little low brazier. The children sit

Imported nail polish and palm oil are sold side by side at the Adjamé market.

on the sandy ground and eat peppered stew out of one common bowl.

There is, however, one difference. Families from twelve different tribes live on Kipré's block. His next-door neighbor is an Agni tribesman from the eastern part of the forest. In the bush, Agnis and Bétés still distrust one another. In the city, their children go to school together, and the old tribal rivalries are slowly disappearing, even among their parents.

Over the years, Kipré has saved enough to be able to buy a record player. This has boosted his social standing among his relatives who visit him from the village and has allowed Kipré to become president of a record club.

For a semieducated young African, Kipré has done well. He has been able to furnish his living room with the comforts every city family wants in order to "keep up." He has been able to get out of the village where he was under the domination of his elders, and because he is able to feed and lodge visiting relatives, he is looked up to by them.

Kipré would certainly not be happy if he went back to live in the village. And yet, at times, he may feel lonely. He may long to hear people speak his tribal language all around him. Once a week he attends a Bété club. There he can meet his "brothers," young men who were boys in villages just like his own.

Though Kipré has learned to adjust to both worlds, he does not seem quite at home in downtown Abidjan. Sometimes, when his workday is over, when the stores have closed and the bats have unhooked their wings from the mango trees to fly into a purple sky, Kipré takes his briefcase and walks home, slowly, past the shops. He stares at the Paris imports he may never be able to buy. Sometimes, he meets the market women carrying home their unsold lettuce and window-shopping, too, and shoeshine boys pressing their noses on the glass panes and arguing which wristwatch is better.

To them, Abidjan is still an unreal world they do not quite belong in. The night watchman in Kipré's office feels this way, too. He is a Mossi tribesman from Upper Volta, and he has brought his bush ways to the city. When he comes to work, he spreads out his goatskin to lie on. He is prepared for everything with his bow and arrows, his flashlight, and a very small transistor radio to keep him awake through the night.

Cargo ships from all over the world line up at Abidjan's harbor.

5

A Country of Planters

"A country that rises is like a growing tree." President Houphouet-Boigny used these words to describe the way he feels about his country's economy. "At all times the planter must take care of it, prune it, make sure not to favor one branch over another . . . so that the tree will produce the best possible fruits." The Ivory Coast has always been a land of farmers. With cautious planning Houphouet-Boigny has maintained its wealth and modernized its farming.

The history of the Ivory Coast's economy and the way in which it has evolved are partly reflected in the story of a family that has grown cocoa for three generations.

Yao Bléwé, an Agni tribesman from the eastern forest, is one of 600,000 dedicated cocoa growers. Every day he goes with six field hands to the family farm. In April he plants the cocoa seedlings in neatly spaced out rows and weeds the overgrowth so that ferns will not choke the young shoots that must grow strong with the May rains. Then he tends to the cocoa trees he planted five years ago. In a few months their pods will ripen to a yellow gold. He trims the trees. He prunes and sprays them. In November when the pods are ready for harvest, Yao starts his day especially early. He leads his family and laborers into the shady grove to cut the pods, put them into baskets, and carry them down the forest path.

Cocoa, being harvested in this forest plantation, and coffee are the Ivory Coast's major export crops.

Once the beans have fermented and dried, Yao will hire a truck and drive into town to sell them. This has been a good year for him. There has been enough rain, and prices for cocoa are expected to be high. He may have hired the mason to build a second floor to his house. He may have ordered the tailor to sew him a new ceremonial gown. This year he may even buy a gold medallion for his wife. He will deposit most of his earnings, however, in the bank.

Back in the village, he will invite neighbors and relatives to celebrate the good year in his compound. He will serve them Scotch and gin and urge them all to drink up, for no one shall say that farmer Yao is not a generous man. But even before the drumming begins, he will ask the chief to pour a few drops of rum on the ground and thank ancestors and earth gods for this year's prosperity.

His granduncle Kwame lived in the same village with his four wives and children. In those days the family raised all its food: yams and cassava, manioc and banana plantains, enough for everyone to eat his fill. If his wives needed meat to enrich their yam stew, the boys would hunt. And when the villagers required a supply of wine, Kwame's older children would climb the palm trees and tap them. There was hardly any need for money. When Kwame wanted a new gun or a lamé cloth for his favorite wife, he would send out servants with a pouch of gold dust and three bags of kola nuts, which they would exchange at the large forest market, a day's walk from the village.

But this quiet way of life stopped when a harsh French governor came to the Ivory Coast in 1908. He had received orders from Paris that no colony should be a financial burden. He was to develop new crops in addition to the timber and the oil of palm that were already being exported. With cocoa and coffee, this colony would make more money and become self-sufficient.

One day the governor's men arrived at Kwame's village. They brought thousands of cocoa seedlings and tried to convince the villagers to plant them. But neither Kwame nor any of his brothers or neighbors showed much interest. Waiting five years for this strange tree to produce was much too long, they complained. Their yams took only a few months to grow. Besides, the daily weeding and pruning the governor's men had told them about, the drying and fermenting of the beans, was much too time-consuming. "Since we cannot eat the fruit of this tree, what good is it to us anyway?" Kwame asked the inspector.

But the governor's men had orders to use force on villagers who resisted. The police brought seedlings and led Kwame and his neighbors into the forest. They made them plant the cocoa in the prescribed space. Every day the guards came back to see that the new plantations were being properly cared for, and they would leave only at sundown.

One night Kwame ordered his wives, children, and grandchildren to go into the forest and pour buckets of boiling water on the young plants. The next morning, the guards returned. When they saw the withered leaves, they rushed to get the inspector so that he could see the damage for himself. He walked into Kwame's compound shouting at the villagers, but Kwame quietly answered him: "We told you it would not grow here."

Some forest tribes closer to the coast had to give in. But in Kwame's village, everyone continued peacefully raising yams. The use of force had been the wrong approach.

Years passed before Kwame realized the advantage of cocoa, and then only when relatives from across the border told him how people all over the Gold Coast forest were becoming wealthy from cocoa. They had planted it ten years ago. As a result, in 1910, the Gold Coast (now known as Ghana) was already exporting twenty thousand tons of cocoa beans, while the neighboring Ivory Coast exported only six tons.

In 1915, Kwame started his cocoa plantation. Soon after, neighbors followed his example. Five years later, in December, Kwame with his sons, nephews, and servants walked ten miles through the forest to a larger village, carrying baskets of beans to sell. This was his first harvest.

The French purchasing agent had set up his scale in the middle of the village, near the store. Next to him stood his interpreter, who translated into the Agni language. Perhaps fifty planters stood around waiting for him to weigh their beans and pay them. It was a long wait, for there were endless arguments. The agent would accuse the planters of having loaded the bottom of their burlap bags with stones or rotten cocoa beans to make them heavier. Then he would make them empty the bags on the ground, and in turn the planters would get angry and accuse the agent, through his interpreter, of using a false scale.

When Kwame was finally paid, he entered the village store. He stood in the small shop hesitating between cotton cloth or a storm lamp. In the store he met important chiefs who had come from nearby villages to sell their first cocoa beans, too. Some of them wore their gold crowns and were closely followed by boy attendants, who carried their scepters and multicolored parasols. To them money was such a new thing that they wore the bills pinned on their togas.

After each harvest, Kwame brought home European goods he had bought with part of his earnings. He would stuff the leftover money into an earthenware jug that he buried in the forest, telling no one where he had put it, not even his own sons.

By the end of the 1920's, those jugs were getting very full indeed. Not only Kwame and his neighbors, but also all the cocoa planters in the country were becoming rich.

When Kwame died, his nephew inherited from him, as was the custom in the tribe. He expanded the plantation, since he could now afford to hire two northern laborers to help him. At the village store he bought European iron beds. From now on, neither he nor his sons would have to sleep on straw mats. In the 1929 harvest season, he replaced his family's straw-thatched roof with a shiny new corrugated one. He was the first villager to open a bank account.

That year a roving reporter came to the Ivory Coast. He had loaded his bags with little mirrors and pocketknives, which he intended to bring as presents to Agni tribal chiefs. He became the laughing stock of the colony, and the French governor himself promptly advised him to repack his trinkets, for these "forest natives" he was to visit by now had nicely padded checkbooks. Some even owned cars.

But all did not go smoothly for even the most successful planters. There were the lean years when prices for cocoa were low. Yao remembers when his uncle would walk home with almost nothing in his pocket. He would sit in a corner of the compound and make bitter remarks about all those months of care for beans that turned out to be nearly worthless. He blamed the governor for the low prices and was convinced that in France his beans were being sold high. There were no drumming parties in those years, and planters

Farmers cut pineapple—a new export crop.

poured a few drops of rum on the ground to beg their ancestors to
relieve them from all this hardship. There was no money to pay the
hired laborers and, what was worse, no money to pay the tax. Yao's
father and uncles had to make up for it by working as forced laborers
on the new road.

Yao was seventeen when his uncle died, in 1945, and he took over
the plantation. Fortunately, the worst of the hard times was over,
but he could remember the years of World War II, when his family

A field hand taps for latex at a new rubber plantation.

had to hand over all their cocoa crop without receiving cash. He could remember how their cocoa rotted on the docks when ships stopped coming altogether, and how lucky they were that his father had continued to grow yams. At least they did not go hungry.

By 1953, when France began to take a new interest in the Ivory Coast, life in the village improved. Yao had children now, and they went to the new school. When they were sick, he took them to the little dispensary that had just been completed. The proudest day of his life was Independence Day. With his three uncles who had been active members of the planters' union, Yao went to the capital and shook hands with the President. He promised that electricity would soon come to their village, together with a new sawmill. When the French flag came down, the President rose to make his first speech as head of the new republic. Yao listened and nodded his head when Houphouet-Boigny reminded everyone that the wealth of this country was in the soil, but that it needed to be developed and enriched with new crops. The President urged the people to realize how fortunate their country was to start out its new life with vast reserves of untouched and promising land. He told them about the European firms that were coming to start enormous banana and palm-oil plantations and the new jobs that would be created. He urged the small farmers to open up more land and plant a second crop in addition to cocoa or coffee, so that when the prices of one crop dropped, they would have another to fall back on. Yao and his uncles looked at each other, for they knew how they had suffered when their cocoa had been sold at ruinous prices.

Now the time had come, the President urged, to improve the cocoa and coffee, to tear out those trees too old to produce good beans and replace them with sugar cane, pineapple, cotton, or palms. Yao liked that advice. After all, the President had been a planter himself before he went into politics. He knew what was best for the country.

And so Yao planted pineapple. He started with a very small field near the cocoa farm, but when the new fruit cannery opened, Yao enlarged his field. It proved well worth it. Three years later he tore down the family's mud house and replaced it by one built with cement bricks. He has been able to send his son to study medicine at the university in the city.

As a result of Yao's efforts and the work of enterprising farmers

A rapidly expanding new industry: deep-sea fishing.

like him, under the wise leadership of the President, this small country, with a population of only 4.4 million, has become the world's fourth largest producer of cocoa, the world's third largest producer of pineapple, the world's third largest producer of coffee, and the world's sixth largest producer of bananas. New industries have been created to use these agricultural products—an instant coffee plant, fruit canneries, textile mills, sawmills, plywood factories, and fish canneries. The Ivory Coast has attained one of the highest per capita incomes of Black Africa.

The fact that the country has remained stable both politically and economically has attracted American interests. For the first time, American banks have made loans to the Ivory Coast for low-cost housing, and the government has helped finance a new dam.

So far, President Houphouet-Boigny has achieved more for his people's well-being than any other African leader. He has been criticized for giving too many posts to European advisers and administrators. To this Houphouet-Boigny answers that these men bring the skills and training that are needed until Ivorians can take over.

The investments he had hoped for have kept on coming in even larger amounts than he had expected. Year after year, production targets have been met. Year after year the economy reaches new peaks, unheard of for any developing country. The obvious question is: if the boom were to stop, what would happen to the people who

Senufo carver mass-produces traditional pieces for the tourist trade.

A new source of income: traditional carvings fetch high prices from European and American collectors.

Cars for the growing middle-class, assembled in Abidjan.

have become used to a good life? Farmers like Yao will always have their land, but the city people who now take many comforts for granted, who have bought new cars, radios, and refrigerators on credit, could be hard hit.

Yet, the boom continues. Even the north and the west, which had remained so far behind the affluent south, are starting to feel the change. And though his country is still unevenly developed, President Houphouet-Boigny expects that there will be no more need for foreign aid by 1970, not a mud hut by 1975, and complete self-sufficiency by 1980.

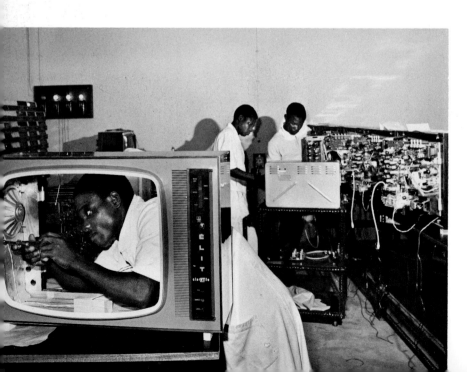

More city families can now afford TV's and radios, locally assembled.

Logs in Abidjan's wood harbor await shipment abroad. Lumber is the country's third major export.

Most students at the university come from affluent forest and coastal regions.

Worlds apart, except for the sewing machine, this savanna village remains a hundred years behind the city.

6

Generation Gap

Far north, five hundred miles from the capital, the Sahara wind blows hot and harsh and dry. Zié, a Senufo tribesman, works his exhausted soil, digging for yams with a primitive hoe. Sanou, eighteen, digs behind his father. They wear coarse loincloths. Their faces carry the Senufo tribe's unmistakable mark: three long streaks cut on either side of the mouth, curved and deep as their fields' furrows, and irremovable. Today these marks have been outlawed by the new government, anxious to erase tribal distinctions and shape the people into one national society.

Year after year Zié has raised yams, and year after year, ever since he was tall enough to lift a hoe, Sanou has helped him. Sanou has always envied his cousin—the only boy in the village allowed to go to school. When Sanou asked the elders if he might attend, they said: "School! That's only for the lazy," and kept him home because they knew he would make a good field worker.

Thirty-three circular huts make up Zié's village in this isolated savanna.

Zié's tribe, like many others in the undeveloped parts of the Ivory Coast, still resists change and fears the progress that is reaching into its world. Last year, for instance, Zié and the elders had to give in and let a medical team vaccinate their cattle. Today the village owns three radios and one sewing machine. But Zié continued to fear change. Every day he saw young social workers crisscrossing the fields on their bicycles, winding around the sacred groves and stopping two villages up the road. He saw them enter the teacher's house, outside the village. He saw the local official going in to meet them and the chief, followed by his advisers.

Had he been there, Zié would not have liked it. He would have heard about the new, large-scale rice fields. He would have heard that the village huts were soon to be torn down and replaced by rectangular cement houses, all neatly aligned along wide, straight lanes. He would have met young women teaching village mothers strange new ways—teaching them to include eggs in their daily diet—eggs that are thrown to the pigs in Zié's tribe for fear they bring bad luck.

If they were asked, the elders in Zié's village would all say no to change. Every time Sanou urged his father to switch from planting yams to planting cotton or rice as the government wanted, Zié said no. "My boy," he answered, "the ancestors would take their revenge if we changed anything on their soil—if we moved as much as one yam mound!" His father would not even let Sanou have a portion of the land to plant as he wanted. No, Sanou would have to wait until he got married and had the help of a wife on the farm. The elders would not even let him choose his own wife; they chose one for him years ago, and now his future father-in-law expected Sanou to plow his field as well.

One day Sanou had had enough of elders. His longing for a life of his own was so strong, he went to the capital hoping to find a job. One of twenty thousand village boys coming to the city every year, he was lucky to find work in a new factory. Being a northerner, he was used to hard manual labor, but he had to learn to get to the factory every day at seven before the siren blew. In the village, no one paid any attention to time. You wakened when the thirsty calves bothered the cows at dawn. You plowed till the shadow of the baobab tree reached the end of the field. In the evenings, you lingered for a while, stretched out in a furrow over a jug of millet beer with friends.

At Konamoukro village, a social worker uses a doll to show Baoulé women modern child-care methods.

To improve village life, illiterate girls learn gardening, poultry care, balanced nutrition, and reading and writing at a government center. Some will train as social workers and teachers.

Teaching what she has learned, nineteen-year-old social worker Marie Tyté takes a youngster to a new kindergarten, where she conducts the class. She also convinces mothers to improve cooking and to include protein-rich eggs in their daily diet.

Primary school students do their homework in a village compound. There are still few secondary schools.

Only one out of 250 schoolchildren has a chance to enter the university. At the new University of Abidjan, Professor Gabriel Johnson discusses a local crab specimen with his zoology class.

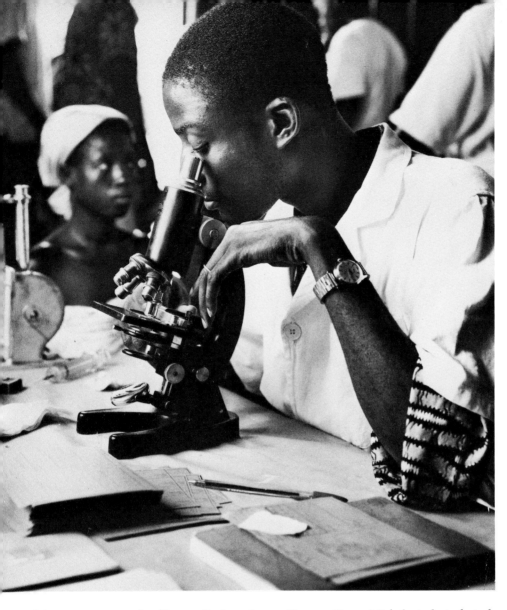

Many young people, like medical assistant Dayoro Boga Michel, study technical
skills at various trade schools.

Only the chief wore a watch in the village to give him prestige, and it had stopped working years ago. But in the city, Sanou needed a watch in order to get to work on time. There were no excuses. No one asked if he was the son of a chief or the son of a slave. It did not matter who he was or what tribe he came from: if he was late, he would be fired.

If he wanted to get ahead in the city, Sanou had to do it on his own. In the village, everything was teamwork: together Sanou and the boys set fish traps in the rivulets, together they cleared the chief's field, together they repaired the thatch on a roof, and when they were twelve, together they were initiated into the tribe. Only because they were together did each one have enough courage, that night, to face the fire-spitting masks encircling them in the moonless grove.

To fight his loneliness in the city, Sanou joined a Senufo club, a sort of miniature tribe. Here he met boys who had recently run away from their elders, and men who had left the tribal society years ago.

One man at the club became a particular friend—Coulibaly, a Senufo tribesman in his sixties and one of the club's founders. Couli-

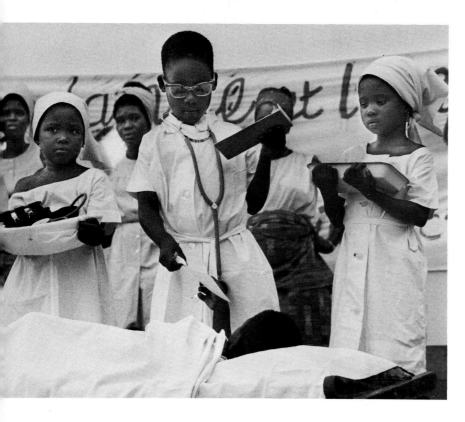

City youngsters play doctor, patient, and nurse in a UNICEF Day skit.

Northern tribesman Bazona Bagnama left the bush to become a pastry chef at an Abidjan hotel.

baly lent Sanou the money to buy himself a watch. He invited him home and listened to him talk about how difficult he found life in Abidjan. Coulibaly always had a kind word for Sanou and assured him that forty years ago it had been even more difficult for a young man to adjust to the city.

Sanou was full of questions. What made Coulibaly persevere? Coulibaly answered: "The fact that we were the first boys in the whole country to enter the Frenchman's world. Only five of us, from the tribe, had gone to school." What had been the hardest problem? For his generation, the greatest problem came when the new law abolished polygamy. Coulibaly had four wives, and the new law recognized only one. This custom had made sense in the village, for

71

Sunday in the city brings capacity crowds to the Houphouet-Boigny sports stadium, where they watch school gymnastics and a soccer match. Fans and policemen share the excitement of the game.

A member of the city elite—Amichia Joseph, a judge in Abidjan.

the more wives and children a man had, the more help he got from them on his farm. But in the city, where a dish of peppered stew cost four times as much as it had in the bush, a man had trouble supporting even one wife and one set of children. Coulibaly was forced to make a heartbreaking decision—which wives was he to send home to their villages? Which wife would he keep? "We all love our husband," one of them said. Another asked: "How can my children grow up without their father?"

At Coulibaly's house Sanou met his son Koné and his young wife Onakem. Sanou was surprised—she was from a different tribe. In the village the elders looked down on mixed tribal marriages, but Onakem and Koné were both born in the city and had gone to school together. Such marriages were not unusual here, they said. In fact, some of Koné's friends who studied in France had come back with French wives. It also surprised Sanou that all these young men were educated. One out of three children now attended school, Koné, who was a lawyer, explained. Right now there were perhaps as many as forty thousand Ivorian students at home and abroad.

A new law that abolished the tribal custom of paying a bride price had made it easier for young men to get married. In his father's time, a man had to pay large sums of money to the bride's father to compensate for the loss of his daughter. In certain tribes where girls were in the minority, this amount could go up to $400, and often only a successful middle-aged man could afford a bride. Young men would sometimes kidnap girls and move off with them to another village.

Today no young man needs to kidnap a girl or go into debt to get married. But even in the city where the bride price no longer needs to be paid, some girls feel that a present ought to be given to their fathers. As Koné's wife admitted, "I would feel cheap if Koné had not 'paid' Father some small thing for me. What would my friends say when they come to visit me from the village? 'See this one: how she scrubs her husband's floor for nothing! How she does his shirts for nothing!' "

There was another new law that Coulibaly and Koné thought well of—the inheritance law. Under most tribal systems, inheritance went from uncle to nephew. Regardless of how many years a son had helped his father on the farm, the nephew would inherit, even if he lived in the city and knew nothing about field work. This created great jealousies, sometimes leading to witchcraft, poisonings, even murder. The new law changed all this: inheritance now goes from father to son, thus bringing the new Ivory Coast society under the same set of laws as the Western world.

75

New life for Zié's village: Sanou enrolls for agricultural training, drives a bulldozer to clear new plots, and harvests his first cotton crop.

An everyday sight in a forest village: children walking to primary school.

Sanou spent many evenings in Coulibaly's home, As time went on, he realized that he did not want to continue working at the factory. He would never get used to it, and being uneducated, he would drift from one factory job to another or perhaps end up, as so many other boys did, jobless and living at some relative's home, ashamed to return to the village.

Coulibaly and his son Koné worked out a plan for Sanou. Koné talked to a man in the Ministry of Education, and a few months later, the minister's aide called Sanou to his office and told him he had been recruited for training in the agricultural program. He explained how every year twenty-five thousand village boys were being trained to become progressive farmers, once their elders had pledged to give them a plot, and how they went back to their villages to grow new crops. The word "bush," he said—with these young farmers' example —was becoming a word of the past.

Sanou liked the idea, but he shook his head. His father would never allow it. But it seemed that Zié had already agreed to give Sanou five acres of land, which he could cultivate after he finished his training in a nearby camp. Six other boys had been recruited from the same village.

For eighteen months Sanou studied the new farming techniques. He learned to grow cotton, tobacco, and rice. He learned about modern poultry and animal husbandry. Sanou also learned to read and write. In the evenings boys from the east exchanged songs and drumbeats with boys from the west, and for the first time Sanou felt that the Senufos and the Lobis and the Wobés belonged to one nation, even though each one had distrusted the other in the past.

A few weeks later Sanou and the six other boys returned with the instructor to the village, and it was Sanou who drove the bulldozer and cleared the new land as the elders stood by. After the plots had been cleared, the boys planted their fields with cotton and went back to camp for the last phase of training. Although they returned several times to see that their cotton grew properly, they did not leave the camp until it was time for their first harvest.

Then Sanou really had something to write Coulibaly about. "Now no one laughs at us any more. Each of us made well over $200 on our first cotton. Imagine—that much money is unheard of here! Zié and the elders still don't admit they were wrong. They still look at us a bit suspiciously, but the chief has decided to plant cotton, too, and he came to me for advice. My father thinks he might just follow his example. Now that the elders are slowly giving up the worn-out ways, now that they, too, want the change, the bush is becoming a good place to live."

7

Heritage

To the sound of tam-tams, somber and strong, the funeral limousine drove slowly past the airport to enter the sacred grove. This was May, 1967, and *this* was no ordinary funeral. Ambassadors from Western countries, presidents of neighboring African republics, the entire Ivory Coast government marched next to Baoulé tribal chiefs and female wailers to pay their last respects to Kimou M'Bra, the deceased aunt of President Houphouet-Boigny.

For ten days the whole country had mourned and brought traditional offerings to the President's family. His aunt's body lay in state, surrounded by gold scepters, crowns, and tribal treasures for the first time publicly displayed. Black-gowned mourners performed the three most sacred tribal dances, never before seen by outsiders. On the tenth day, cannons were fired as the bier was lowered into the ground. The dead aunt was awarded the highest honor of the land as her nephew named her Grand Officer of the National Order.

This was the country's first official tribal event. It seemed surprising, for the Ivory Coast had up to now played down its African heritage as it attempted to modernize the country. When the funeral was over, a reporter asked the President to justify the lavish ceremony, especially since he had campaigned against such outdated and

Historian Adiko Assoi tapes legends of an Akan chief.

costly practices as no longer fitting the new African way of life. Houphouet-Boigny replied that his aunt had been a second mother to him and had made great sacrifices for him in her lifetime. She had resigned herself to the new law abolishing old and sacred tribal customs on the condition that he would, one day, honor her with a funeral worthy of a tribal queen.

Until very recently the Ivory Coast minimized its heritage, a neglect dating back to colonial times. When the French took over the country, they imposed their culture, their religion. They took African children to school by force, stripped them of their loincloths and juju charms, put them into khaki uniforms, and taught them French—a completely foreign language. They taught them to add and substract with examples of apples and pears that did not grow in Africa. The first sentence of their history books read: "Our ancestors the Gauls," and they pretended that these African boys had no past of their own. Besides, schoolchildren were kept from attending tribal ceremonies that most colonizers considered "barbarian."

The first generation of educated Ivorians was eager to enter the Frenchman's world, to obtain administrative jobs, and they, too, played down their African background. If they participated in tribal ceremonies, they would not talk about them.

It was the outside world that made the Ivory Coast realize it had been neglecting its heritage far too long. This happened when the 1966 African Arts Festival in Senegal honored the entire continent's artistic contributions, when Afro-Americans started to search into their African past, when France and the United States turned to Africa with a new interest in its art, and when new anthropologists came to study the Ivory Coast's tribes.

Suddenly, Ivorians realized that their rich heritage was fast slipping away. Gradually, a reverse trend set in. The elite felt that something had to be done to record and give new meaning to this heritage. A few years ago the Ivorian author Bernard Dadié wrote interpretations of tribal legends, and an Ivorian anthropologist initiated research into his tribal background, regretting that his own students at the university would still rather study Latin American Indians than go back to their grandfathers' village with a tape recorder. Textbooks have been rewritten to introduce Ivorian students to their past, and they have been taken on museum tours where they can see, for the first time, tribal carvings their parents would not have shown

In the bush, city girls carry food offerings and plastic schoolbags to initiation rites. In the city museum, they view tribal carvings.

them. Perhaps this new national trend may have changed the way Ivorians regard their background. Perhaps now the ceremonies in the sacred groves, the tribal dances, are being talked about more openly, at least within the families.

When young people in the city are old enough, a grandfather may request their presence in the bush. On this first visit, the city youngsters are somewhat apprehensive. They may speak French more fluently than the tribal language. They may have trouble, at first, understanding Grandmother. In her compound they must eat foufou, the boiled yam dish, while they are more used to French food and the bottled drinks they get in school. But slowly, a whole new world will open up to them. For the first time they will meet the chief. They will see the villagers treat this illiterate old man with great respect, and they, too, will have to bow or kneel in the sand in his presence and call him "Nana." They may be taken by an older cousin from compound to compound to be introduced, and as they meet the jeweler, the fishermen, the carver, the planters, and the white-robed fetish priest, they may begin to perceive that in this tight-knit community, everyone, down to the poorest, is treated with dignity, that no one is left out.

Traditions are maintained in the village: a city youngster learns to play an old checkers game and the drums.

When they are old enough to participate in the initiation ceremony, the grandfather may, once more, request their presence, for he is convinced that if children do not spend more time watching and learning the old ways, they will grow up lacking the right human qualities. In many communities, however, initiations that used to last several years have been shortened to just a few weeks, to fit them into the city children's school vacation.

When Brigitte and Gabriel Kwassi go back to the village to be initiated, they will find the ceremonies strange. They will hear songs in a ritual language they do not understand. They will be told only a small part of the old beliefs. Each one will be guided and sponsored by an older village cousin who may paint Brigitte's face with white makeup—the color of purity and of the gods—wrap her in a yellow satin robe, and teach her to swing her arms high and twirl a fly whisk so she can join the village girls in the coming-out dance. Her brother Gabriel may be asked to participate in the warrior dance. In the old days its purpose was to gather young warriors who defended the village from attack by enemy tribes. The young men who participated in this dance used swords and guns. Today Gabriel will carry a branch or a stick and learn to shout old war cries as he escorts the adult "captain" who wears leopard skins and a tall, mirrored headdress. Even though the warrior dance has lost its original purpose, it still rallies to the village young men who have been away for years. In fact, important members of the government have often removed their striped suits and put on the leopard costume for the occasion.

Once Gabriel has participated in the warrior dance, he is accepted by the villagers as a member of their community. The old village carver may ask him to come to his forest retreat and watch him shape a dance mask. Gabriel has seen similar carvings in the city museum, but now he may learn from the carver that each mask still has a purpose and serves the community in a religious or a social way. Gabriel may also learn that a mask worn by a dancer in a ceremony acquires supernatural powers; it may settle a quarrel; it may punish a thief; it may even succeed in getting the gods to stop the rains or the drought. Later, Gabriel will be allowed to watch the masked dancers in the forest. Then he will hear the voice coming out of that mask, thin, shrill, and eerie, resembling something from the spirit world.

As young adults, Gabriel and his sister may return to share important moments in their lives with their village families. Gabriel may be called upon to represent his father at the yam festival. After Brigitte has married, she may return to present her first child to the grandparents. The relatives will gather to choose a tribal name for the child. Then the young mother will smear her body with white paint, wrap herself in a tribal gown, and carry her newborn from compound to compound, where each family will slip a present of money into her large city handbag.

Obligations to attend tribal ceremonies in the village conflict with the modern African's job and new way of life. Django, thirty-four years old and a successful car salesman in Abidjan, explained: "If my uncle is ill, I must return to the village and be with him, for he brought me up in the traditions. My kinsfolk would never understand why I cannot leave the job for a few days and come home. As for my boss (a Frenchman)—he obviously does not understand. In his society, an uncle is unimportant. . . . How can I make him realize that missing these ceremonies might get me dishonored in my tribe? . . . Unfortunately, the Europeans expect us to behave their way at all times. To them tribal events are childish. How little do they know our way of life! How little do they know us!"

Django is a dedicated employee of his firm. Yet, he has made up his mind about leading part of his life as an educated city African and the rest as a member of a tribal community. "Education, a job, a modern skill allow us to earn a decent living. But when the office closes at five—where do we stand? We cannot live entirely their way. We cannot break our ties with our world. After all—some of us might want to grow old in the village."

Some educated Africans try to combine the best of both worlds. Those whose villages are close enough to the city keep a village home where they return on weekends. Others, like Albert Topé, a fifty-two-year-old Abouré tribesman and a high school teacher, decide to return to the village for good after having spent twenty or thirty years in the city. When they do, they bring new ways with them and try to improve the life of their village communities.

Albert Topé went back to the same compound he grew up in as a boy. He has modernized it but has remembered always to keep an empty room for a widow, an orphan, or some relative in need.

Surrounded by painted animal totems of his clan, an Abouré village elder passes on folktales to the young.

The coastal Harris cult blends elements of Christianity, Islam, and Animism to appeal to African needs. Preacher Atcho welcomes a convert, hears confessions of witchcraft, and conducts a service in dialect, assisted by priests outfitted with Moslem gowns and Catholic crosses.

Part of the heritage is preserved: the art of carving is carried on by a young Senufo artist.

His years in the city have not erased in him the basic African tradition of hospitality. On some nights the chief and the elders bring their storm lamps and their wooden stools to Topé's compound. While they watch the young people dance, the chief and Topé will talk about their future. "See this boy?" Topé says. "He might well end up at the university, but that one—it would be best if he stayed with us, on the plantation."

Topé has ambitions for his family and for the entire community. While supporting a young brother through business school and a son who is a doctor in Abidjan, Topé has formed a cooperative in the village to enable the farmers to share equipment. He has convinced the elders to cut down on funeral expenses and use this money instead to send three promising youngsters to study in Abidjan. Soon the village will start building a dispensary with a fund initiated by Topé and enriched by contributions from relatives in the city.

Every Sunday friends from bush and city gather at Topé's compound. The village teacher comes to hear news from the city, to borrow Topé's books, or to discuss politics with his relatives who have jobs in the ministries. The illiterate chief comes to listen to Topé's radio and often will ask him for financial advice. The city visitors come to bask in the peaceful ways of the village. In the evening, dressed in a flowing gold and green gown, Topé tells the young boys the tribal legends—perhaps about the Abourés' long and painful exile from the Ashanti warriors in the eighteenth century, perhaps about how Queen Pokou had to sacrifice her child so the river would let the fleeing tribesmen cross, perhaps about the day his great-grandfather fired on the French brig that sailed up their river a century ago. And Topé may do as his great-grandfather did when he tells this tale: he may touch his eyes, meaning, "I know. These eyes have seen."

No listener dozes off while Topé speaks. When he finishes one tale, the boys crouched next to him pull at his robe and request yet another, for Topé brings to life the commonest animal tales, the grumbling elephants of the forest, the impertinent hyena with her mocking laughter, and the crocodile gnashing his teeth and swishing in the sand.

Encouraged by friends in the Ministry of Education, Topé has started to write about his tribe's past. Sometimes he travels to a

remote forest village, where a very old tribesman can still tell him about an event no one else remembers. As his work grows, Topé sees his tribe's heritage in perspective. He sees that some customs have disappeared, for they no longer belong to the new way of life. Others, he sees, are essential to preserve for those young people who have grown away from the village, for his own sons and grandsons who still return to participate in important ceremonies. As his work takes shape, Topé sees that the timeless African values have remained: the compassion for people in need, the hospitality, the respect for old age, the basic sense of justice, and also the gaiety of heart, for as Topé himself reminds the young, "Let us not give up our sense of humor for imported ideas of happiness. *We* still know best how to laugh!"

Topé who has lived in both worlds sees that tribal society has much to say not only to those who have left the village, not only to those who have become too Westernized to remember the old values, but perhaps to people in other countries as well.

A mask covers the dancer's face as he prepares to participate in a Dan tribal ceremony.

Index

Numbers in boldface refer to photographs.

Abidjan, **10,** 25, 31, 32, 35, 37, 39-46, 87, 93
Accra, 39
Agni, 49, 52
Akan tribes, 18
Ashanti, 18
Assinie, King Peter of, 15

Baoulé, 32, 81
Berlin Conference Treaty, 23
Bété, 43
Binger, Louis-Gustave, 23, 24
Bouet-Villaumez, 18

Dadié, Bernard, 82
Dahomey, 21
De Gaulle, Charles, 25, 27, 31, 32, 34

France, 15, 18, 21, 23, 24, 25, 27, 32, 33, 34, 35, 36, 37, 54, 82
Franco-German War, 23

Ghana (formerly Gold Coast), 7, 8, 9, 10, 11, 12, 18, 21, 23, 31, 34, 51
Guinea, 7, 8, 9, 12, 23, 34, 35, 40

Harris cult, **90, 91**
Houphouet-Boigny, Félix, 10, 11, 12, **26,** 31, 32, 33, 34, 35, 37, 40, 49, 54, 55, 56, 58, 81, 82
Houphouet-Boigny, Thérèse, **35**

Lagos, 39
Latrille, André, 31, 33
Liberia, 7, 23
Louis-Philippe I, King, 15

Mali, 7, 8, 34
Map, **8**

Nigeria, 8, 9, 21
Nkrumah, Kwame, 10, 11, 12

Peace Corps, 8
Péchoux, Laurent, 33
Pétain, Marshall, 25

Senegal, 9, 34, 82
Senghor, Leopold, 34
Senufo, 61
Slave trade, 18, 21

Touré, Samory, 23
Touré, Sekou, 34

United Nations, 35
United States, 36, 82
University of Abidjan, **60, 68**
Upper Volta, 7

Verdier, Arthur, 21, 23
Vietnam, 32

World War II, 24, 27, 53